Top Dog

The Doberman Pinscher

by William R. Sanford and Carl R. Green

CRESTWOOD HOUSE

New York

CIP

LIBRARY OF CONGRESS CATALOGING IN PUBLICATION DATA

Sanford, William R. (William Reynolds)
  Doberman pinscher

  (Top dog)
  Includes index.
  SUMMARY: Discusses the history, physical characteristics, care, and breeding of this highly intelligent dog frequently used for protection.
  1. Doberman pinschers — Juvenile literature. [1. Doberman pinschers. 2. Dogs.] I. Green, Carl R. II. Title. III. Series: Sanford, William R. (William Reynolds), Top dog.
SF429.D6S36   1989   636.7'3 — dc20   89-31071
ISBN 0-89686-454-5

PHOTO CREDITS

Cover: Reynolds Photography: Larry Reynolds
Animals Animals: (Robert Pearcy) 4; (Zig Leszczynski) 34; (George Roos) 39; (Michael & Moppet Reed) 42
Animal Humane Society: (Nils Anderson) 21
DRK Photo: (Don & Pat Valenti) 30
FPG International: (Adolf Schmidecker) 24
Photo Researchers, Inc.: (Carolyn A. McKeone) 10
Reynolds Photography: (Larry Reynolds) 7, 12, 15, 18, 37

CRESTWOOD HOUSE

Macmillan Publishing Company
866 Third Avenue
New York, NY 10022
Collier Macmillan Canada, Inc.

Produced by Carnival Enterprises

Printed in the United States of America

First Edition

10 9 8 7 6 5 4 3 2 1

TABLE OF CONTENTS

FOR MORE INFORMATION

For more information about Doberman pinschers, write to:

American Kennel Club
51 Madison Avenue
New York, NY 10010

Doberman Pinscher Club of
America
22371 Sequoia Circle
Lake Elsinoie, CA 92330

A WIN FOR A DOBERMAN DRILL TEAM

Donna Farrell dropped her pom-poms on the floor and fell into an easy chair. She looked tired and unhappy.

Mrs. Farrell looked up from her book. "I can see things didn't go well at the parade," she said. "Tell me about it."

Donna pulled off her boots and wiggled her feet. "It's bad enough that my drill team came in second," she said. "What upsets me is that we lost to a team of dogs!" She paused when she saw her mother's surprised look. "Well, the winning team was half teenagers and half Doberman pinschers," she explained.

Mrs. Farrell nodded. "The parade was on television. I could hear the cheers when the Dobermans marched past. I counted twenty dogs, each with a handler. A drill captain led the way, and there were four flag bearers behind them."

"What were the dogs doing?" Donna asked. "We were near the front of the parade, and I couldn't see them."

The Doberman pinscher is a smart dog that can be taught many tricks, including marching and performing in a drill team.

"Those dogs did everything but sing the national anthem," Mrs. Farrell said smiling. "They jumped through hoops and kept their places perfectly. One of them carried an egg in its mouth and never came close to cracking it!"

"I saw the dogs after the parade," Donna said. "Their handlers were wearing blazers, and the dogs had matching coats. They looked sharp! One of the girls told me they've won in almost all of the parades they've entered."

"The TV announcer gave us some history," Mrs. Farrell said. "The first Doberman drill team was organized in California in 1968. It performed at schools, hospitals, and dog shows all over the state. The teams surprise people who have the wrong idea about Dobermans. After seeing them perform, no one can possibly think they're a vicious breed."

"I'm surprised the dogs weren't spooked by the crowd," she said. "My team is always losing step because of something that happens along the way."

"Every dog has been to obedience school," Mrs. Farrell explained. "Some of the dogs have won prizes in *obedience trials*."

"Did the dogs do any unusual tricks?" Donna asked.

"Yes, indeed!" her mother said. "At one

During an obedience trial, Dobermans must closely follow their handlers' commands.

point, some men lined up six cardboard barrels. They must have measured fifteen feet from end to end. One of the Dobermans took a run and jumped over all six barrels!"

"I wish I'd seen it," Donna said. "What else did they do?"

"When they reached the judges' stand, the dogs formed a circle," Mrs. Farrell went on. "Then the handlers dropped their leashes and told the dogs to stay. They walked out, formed a circle of their own, and bowed to the judges.

The crowd was yelling and screaming, but the dogs sat like statues."

Donna smiled at her mother. "Well, at least we didn't lose to an all-human drill team," she said. "Before we compete against Doberman pinschers again, I'm going to find out more about them. They're interesting dogs."

LOUIS DOBERMANN CREATES A NEW BREED OF DOG

Louis Dobermann lived in the little German town of Apolda in the mid-1800s. He held many jobs, including tax collector, town butcher, and dogcatcher. At night, he put on his police officer's uniform and patrolled the town streets. Dobermann loved dogs, and he *bred* them as a hobby. A butcher, he had plenty of food for his animals. A dogcatcher, he could choose from a variety of dogs for his experiments.

Dobermann's plan was to breed the perfect

guard dog. He wanted a large, terrier-type animal that would be fearless, intelligent, and easy to train. Dobermann *crossbred* dogs he thought would pass on these qualities to their *puppies.* By the 1890s, his fierce guard dogs were in great demand. One of Dobermann's friends hid money in his dog's collar when he traveled. He said a bandit would be crazy to try to steal from one of Dobermann's guard dogs.

Dobermann died in 1895, but others carried on his work. Otto Göller, also of Apolda, liked the breed's alert intelligence and its guard-dog *instincts.* At the same time, he wanted to calm the dog's fierce nature. His breeding experiments were successful. His early Dobermans were much smaller than today's dogs. They turned into good house dogs and became one of Germany's most popular breeds.

In 1899, the breed was named the *Dobermannpinscher* in honor of Louis Dobermann. In English, the name means "Dobermann's terrier" (*pinscher* is German for terrier). Outside of Germany, people called the dog the Dobermann pinscher. The British shortened the name to Dobermann in 1949 because Dobermans are clearly *not* terriers. A true terrier is a smaller dog, one that "goes to earth" after rabbits and other game. When the breed reached the United States, Americans kept the full name, but along the way, the last "n" was dropped from Dobermann's name.

Sadly, the early breeders did not keep records of their experiments. Experts can trace the Doberman's origins to several breeds, however. Dobermann probably started by crossing the smooth-coated German shepherd with the Manchester terrier. From the Manchester the Doberman inherited its rich rust red markings. Dobermans also show traces of

the rottweiler, English greyhound, German pointer, and the Great Dane.

By 1904, Dobermans had been exported to Holland, and by 1907 they were in Russia. Germany accepted them as a separate breed in 1911. The breed became popular in the United States after World War I. Among their other roles, Dobermans made fine guide dogs for the blind. The larger, sleeker Doberman developed after breeders imported some breeding stock from Russia. Today, the alert, intelligent Doberman pinscher is the fifteenth most popular dog in the United States.

THE DOBERMAN IN CLOSE-UP

As Louis Dobermann, a town butcher, knew, dogs are meat-eating mammals, or *carnivores*. Scientists place them in the order *Carnivora*. Their family is the *Canidae*, which they share with wolves, foxes, and jackals. All domestic dogs, from tiny toys to tall Dobermans, belong to the same species, *Canis familiaris*.

Today, the Doberman pinscher is the fifteenth most popular dog in the United States.

11

Ever since Dobermann created his first "model," Doberman fanciers have worked to breed a taller, better-looking dog. Fully grown male Dobermans average 27 inches at the *withers* (the top of the shoulder). Female dogs average 1.5 inches less. From chest to rump, a show-quality Doberman should be as long as it is tall. A small Doberman weighs about 50 pounds, while the largest tips the scales at 75 pounds.

The Doberman's colors feature a black coat with rust-colored markings. The rust color appears above the eyes and on the *muzzle*, throat, and forechest. It also can be found on all four legs and below the tail. Less common are reddish brown, blue, and tan-colored dogs. Whatever the color, the short coat should be smooth and thick.

Even at rest, the Doberman looks alert, powerful, and intelligent. The head is long and wedge shaped. The top of the skull is flat, as are the muscular cheeks. The dog's firm lips lie tightly against the jaw. Black Dobermans have black noses, but lighter-colored dogs have dark brown or dark gray noses. Most dogs have round eyes, but a Doberman's deep-set eyes are almond shaped. The eyes are usually medium to dark brown in color.

When the Doberman yawns, it reveals an

A Doberman with a reddish brown coat is not seen as often as a black Doberman.

impressive set of teeth. Puppies begin to cut their 28 baby teeth during the third week after birth. These needle-sharp teeth are replaced by 42 permanent teeth when the dogs are four months old. The Doberman has 6 *incisors* (for cutting), 2 *canines* (for holding and tearing), and 12 *premolars* and *molars* (for slicing and crushing) in the upper jaw. The lower jaw contains 2 extra molars. When a Doberman closes its strong jaws, the teeth meet neatly in a true scissors bite.

Food doesn't last long in those mighty jaws. Like other dogs, Dobermans gulp their food as soon as the chunks are small enough to swallow. The dog's saliva mixes with stomach acids to begin digestion.

All Dobermans have their tails *docked* (cut), and many have their ears *cropped* (shortened). The tail is docked when the puppy is only a few days old. The cut is made at the first or second joint, and leaves only a short stump. The practice goes back to the breed's early history as a guard dog. Dobermann knew that his dogs would be helpless if a thief grabbed them by their tails. Once the tails were docked, the threat disappeared.

Ears are cropped to make them stand erect and give the Doberman its alert look. Otherwise, the Doberman's large ears would droop like those of a hound. Some states, such as New York and Pennsylvania, make it illegal to crop a dog's ears. For that reason, judges do not mark a dog down for having floppy ears. Cropping is usually done by a *veterinarian* when the puppy is about 12 weeks old.

People who love the Doberman think it's the most beautiful of all dogs. The proud, narrow head is carried on a strong, arched neck. The back slopes from withers to hindquarters in a straight, lovely line. The *forelegs* are straight, and the hind legs are powerful. Watch a Doberman running at full speed. It's always in balance and always full of life.

Owners sometimes crop their Dobermans' ears to make them stand erect.

DOBERMANS HAVE KEEN SENSES

Doberman owners like to call the breed "the dog with the human brain." They tell many stories of Dobermans whose quick action saved lives and property. The barking of one Doberman, for example, warned his owner that some electric wiring was on fire. Thanks to the dog, the house was saved from serious damage. The amazing part of the story is that there was a log fire burning in the same room. Somehow, the Doberman knew the difference between a "safe" fire and a dangerous one!

Can Dobermans really think as well as humans? An adult dog's brain weighs only about four ounces. An average human brain weighs three pounds. That doesn't allow much room for high-level thinking. No matter what proud dog owners say, their pets strike out when it comes to problems a child can solve. A scientist proved this by teaching a dog to get food by pushing a lever. Later, the scientist removed the lever. Even though the lever was gone, the dog kept pawing the air where it had been.

16

Dobermans also see the world differently. Dogs do have a wider angle of vision than humans do, but their close-up vision is poor. They detect motion well but may fail to recognize something that isn't moving. When out for a walk, if the neighbor's cat doesn't move, your dog might not see it. Although they are color-blind, dogs do have excellent night vision. They also have a third eyelid, called the *haw*.

At birth, a puppy is both blind and deaf. It can't hear its mother's growls until it is 10 or 12 days old. After that slow start, an adult Doberman develops hearing that is superior to a human's in three ways. The dog can hear higher tones and detect fainter sounds. It also can locate the source of sounds with greater accuracy. The human ear can't hear sounds that go much above 20,000 cycles a second. Dogs respond to high-pitched "silent" whistles at 30,000 cycles a second.

In the sense of smell Dobermans leave humans far behind. This important canine sense depends upon nerve cells (*olfactory patches*) in the nose. Dogs have much larger olfactory patches with many more nerve endings. The most interesting smells to a dog are sweat, blood, urine, and decaying meat. To a dog, the

A Doberman's powerful sense of smell makes it an excellent tracker.

sense of taste is mostly made up of scent, not flavor. That's why a dog will gulp down a foul-tasting medicine as long as it is odorless.

When a Doberman sniffs at a tree stump, it is "reading" a canine "newspaper." The dog can tell if the dogs that passed there earlier were male or female, sick or well, fully fed or hungry. If the dog was a female, the dog knows whether or not she was in *heat,* ready to mate. On command, a trained Doberman can track any of the dogs to its home. Shown an article of your clothing, it can track you through the woods or along a busy city street.

This powerful sense of smell makes up for the dog's less developed senses of taste and touch. Stroke your Doberman's back, though, and watch the reaction. It knows your touch, and it likes the reassuring pressure of your hand.

PEOPLE HAVE THE WRONG IDEA

The public has more wrong ideas about the Doberman pinscher than about any other breed. The problem most likely begins with the Doberman's use as a guard dog. People see Dobermans patrolling or standing watch inside factory gates and other protected areas. As a result, they tend to think of Dobermans only as "attack dogs."

The truth is a little different. Today's Dobermans are not born to be aggressive guard dogs. Like all dogs, they can be taught to attack, and some have been trained that way. Most Dobermans, however, have been firmly and lovingly trained. Properly handled, they are fine family pets. If a Doberman barks when you walk by its house, it's only defending its territory. When its owner says you're a friend, the dog will accept you as one.

Owning a Doberman isn't a simple job. Everyone in the family must share in the care and training of the dog. A Doberman respects discipline, but it will not accept abuse. Although the dog is good with children, it has little patience for teasing. In addition, owners should remember Dobermans are large, active dogs. They need attention and exercise. A dog that is kept in an apartment or in a small backyard will soon become bored. That's often when bad behavior starts.

Another common story is that dogs with narrow heads are stupid. Anyone who is familiar with Dobermans knows how silly that story is! After a hundred years of careful breeding, the Doberman is quick-witted and intelligent. It responds quickly to its owner's wishes and adjusts well to new situations. Even if a Doberman is hot on the trail of a rabbit, it will break off the chase and return on command. If trained as a hunter, it learns quickly to find and retrieve game. Back home, the dog can perform any number of tasks around the house. Do you want your dog to bring in the newspaper and fetch your slippers? The Doberman loves to be of service.

Even though a Doberman is naturally fearless, it doesn't pick fights. If another dog threatens its family, however, look out! No dog is more loyal or protective. As a bonus, the Doberman has great beauty, alertness, and unlimited energy. Like an actor, the Doberman is ready to play any role. It can be the aggressive guard dog—or it can be the loyal family pet. You'll have to decide on the role you want your dog to play.

Because of the demand for Dobermans, a

Although many owners use their dogs as guard dogs, properly trained Dobermans are great family pets.

few breeders sell puppies that have severe defects. These substandard dogs have roached (bent) backs, weak lower jaws, and bad hindquarters. These and similar problems develop in any breed when it starts to sell too well.

CHOOSING THE PERFECT PUPPY

You've thought about it, and you're certain that the Doberman is the perfect dog for you. Most Doberman owners would agree with you. Even so, you shouldn't buy the first dog you see. It's safer to do some planning before you start shopping.

Here are the most popular questions asked by buyers—and the experts' answers:

Where can I find the best puppy? You can find a good puppy at a pet store or at a breeder's kennels. Along with selling you a puppy, a pet store can furnish you with supplies, books, and helpful advice. Most pet stores, however, will have only one or two dogs to show you. A breeder can show you one or more *litters.*

That gives you a better chance of finding a puppy that's "just right." The breeder will be able to tell you about the puppy's parents, and you can look over the dog's *pedigree*. That's important, because heart problems and cancer run in some Doberman family lines. Whether you buy from a pet store or a breeder, be sure your dog is guaranteed. Many sellers will replace your puppy if it is diseased or doesn't adjust well to your family.

How much will I have to pay? If you want to show your dog, buy a puppy that's as nearly perfect as possible. A show-quality Doberman can cost $750 and up. Unless you're already an expert, you'll need help in choosing a dog that has a chance of developing into a champion. Dogs of this quality are usually not sold until they're at least four months old. By that age, you can see if they're going to grow into *show dogs*. If you are content with a pet-quality dog, you can buy a puppy for $350 to $600. The flaws that keep most of these dogs from winning blue ribbons are nearly invisible.

Should I buy a male or female puppy? As a rule, males are a little cheaper, but females make better house dogs. Both sexes can be trained as guard dogs. The advantage of buying a female is that you can breed her and have puppies of your own. Females come into heat twice a year. That's the three-week period when the *bitch* (as a female is called) is ready to be bred. Male dogs know when a female is in heat, so be ready to keep your bitch locked up at these times.

All puppies are cute. How do I pick the right one? Many people fall in love with the first puppy that licks their nose. The experts say you shouldn't let your heart make the choice. First, look for a happy-go-lucky puppy that isn't spooked by strangers. Pick it up and ex-

Look closely at a puppy's parents before buying it. A puppy will usually grow up to look and act a lot like its parents.

amine the puppy carefully. Look for bright, clear eyes and a moist, clean nose. The puppy's belly shouldn't be swollen. It should be chubby without being fat. If the ears have been cropped, make sure they're well shaped and erect. By eight or nine weeks, the puppy will have had its shots and be ready to go home with you. Younger puppies still need their mother and their littermates. Soon after you take the puppy home, have it checked by your vet. If all goes well, you're ready to begin the adventure of training your new pet.

TRAINING YOUR DOBERMAN PINSCHER

What a great day! You've come back from the kennels with a lively Doberman puppy. If you and your new puppy are going to be happy together, you'll have to train it to be well behaved. Luckily, your dog will want to please you. It will also want the security of knowing its place in the family "pack." If a well-meaning friend says to wallop your dog every time it misbehaves, ignore the advice.

Too much punishment can turn your dog into a mean, unhappy dog. Train it with a firm, loving hand and plenty of rewards. This will create a strong bond between the two of you.

Here are some rules for you to use with your new puppy:

Always use the dog's name when you speak to it. It'll soon know its name and will respond.

Never vary the way you give a command. If you start by saying, "Come," don't switch later to "Here, boy." You can *reinforce* the "Come" command by letting the puppy roam on a long rope. If it doesn't come when you call, yank on the rope. After you do this three or four times, your puppy will get the idea.

Always praise your dog when it obeys and always scold it when it misbehaves. You can reinforce good behavior with a dog biscuit, but praise and a pat on the head work just as well.

Dobermans don't learn a new command the first time they hear it. Be patient and repeat the command over and over. If you're teaching your dog to sit, be ready to work on the command for several weeks. Remember, it's hard for an active dog to sit when it wants to run.

Once you give a command, make sure your dog obeys. If it learns that it can ignore you, you've lost the game.

Learning should be fun for both of you. Take time off from training for a game of tag or a wrestling match.

Be sure your dog finishes one task before starting on another. Its brain can't process too many things at one time.

Here are two situations where you can apply these rules. *Housebreaking* your dog—teaching it not to relieve itself in the house—will be one of your first tasks. Confine it in its kennel when you're not working or playing with it. Instinct will keep it from soiling its own bed. When you let it out, take it to the place you want it to use. Praise the dog when it performs well. If it has an accident, scold it and mop up the area to remove the odor. Your dog will soon get the picture.

Taking your dog for a walk shouldn't be one long tug-of-war. Start it on a soft nylon lead. When it's three months old, switch to a *choke chain*. The goal is to teach it to heel—to walk quietly at your left side. If your dog dashes after a cat, hold on tightly. The heavy links of the chain will cut off its air. When it relaxes, release the pressure. Drag the dog along for a while if you must. When it heels properly, give it a reward. Both of you will soon be looking forward to your walks.

CARING FOR YOUR DOBERMAN

A Doberman looks to its owner for all of its care. Along with love and discipline, a dog needs a good diet, proper *grooming,* a vet, a warm place to sleep, and exercise.

Ask ten dog owners about diet and you'll likely get ten different answers. Some owners feed their Dobermans dry, packaged dog food. Others depend on canned foods. A few owners prepare fresh meats and vegetables for their dogs. Whichever food you choose, a dog needs a balanced diet. A 5-pound puppy eats about 6 ounces of dry dog food a day. As a 70-pound adult, the same dog will consume 28 ounces of food a day. A puppy eats five times a day, but this can be cut to three meals after a few months. At one year, a puppy becomes an adult dog. From then on, it does well on a single big meal each day.

Knowing what *not* to feed a Doberman is also important. Any bone that splinters is dangerous, because it may stick in the dog's throat. Chicken and fish bones are the worst of all. Even though Dobermans have a sweet tooth, candy is another no-no. Sweets increase the risk of cavities and make the dog fat. Also, eating sweets may spoil the dog for its regular diet.

Some people forget that shorthaired dogs need grooming, too. Dobermans shed twice a year, usually in the spring and fall. A regular brushing removes loose hair and keeps the skin healthy. Keep a careful watch on the Doberman's ears and toenails. If its ears become dirty or clogged, clean them with a cotton swab. Nails tend to grow too long when the dog hasn't had enough exercise on hard surfaces. Long nails must be trimmed, but don't cut them yourself unless you've been trained. Cutting into the quick (the pink area of the nail) is painful to the dog.

Most dogs have their shots for *distemper* and other puppy diseases before they're sold. Even so, a Doberman should visit the vet on a regular schedule. The most common problems that vets see are fleas and *worms*. Treat fleas with sprays, powders, flea collars, and shampoos. If these don't work, the vet may have to dip the dog in a flea-killing bath. Worms are parasites that live in the dog's intestines. Dogs with worms develop pot bellies, vomit, and have runny eyes. Along with deworming a

Dobermans, like most other dogs, need plenty of exercise to keep them healthy.

dog, the vet can check for the crippling hip and knee conditions that are common to Dobermans. Medicines can ease the pain, but surgery helps only if the joints are not too badly damaged.

A Doberman needs a warm, dry place to sleep and plenty of exercise. A three-by-four-foot doghouse is about the right size. Raise the doghouse off the ground to avoid drafts and line it with straw or old blankets. A Doberman that's forced to sleep on a hard surface will wear bald spots on its legs.

Take the dog out each day for play and a good run. The exercise is important, but so is the social contact. More than most dogs, Dobermans need to spend lots of time with people.

RAISING DOBERMAN PUPPIES

"Mistel is over a year old now," Alex reminded his parents during dinner. "I think it's time to breed her. With her pedigree, she should produce excellent puppies."

"Raising puppies is a lot of work," Mr. Ford reminded his son. "And if you're thinking about getting rich, forget it. By the time you pay all the costs, you'll be lucky to break even."

"I know that," Alex said. "Even if I don't make any money, it'll still be fun. Look, I've made up a list of what I have to do. I've already found a *stud male*. The Pulitzer Kennels have a champion Doberman that will be perfect. I can pay the stud fee by giving Mr. Pulitzer the pick of the litter."

"I guess you've done your homework," Mr. Ford admitted.

Alex knew he was winning the debate. "I already know that Mistel is in perfect health. The next time she comes into heat, I'll take her to the kennels on the thirteenth day. Once she's mated, I can bring her home. If she's pregnant, all we have to do is wait for nine weeks. If she isn't, I'll take her back for another mating when she goes into heat again."

"Will she need a special diet?" Mrs. Ford wondered.

"She'll need lots of protein and some extra vitamins," Alex said. "Also, I'll have her checked by Dr. Vincent. He'll tell me if she needs anything else. Oh, and I'll give her plenty of mild exercise."

Alex's plan went like clockwork. Three weeks after Mistel was mated, Dr. Vincent confirmed she was pregnant. As the weeks went by, the Doberman's abdomen bulged with unborn puppies. With his dad's help, Alex built a *whelping* box for the coming birth. As the eighth week began, he let Mistel get used to sleeping in the box.

Finally, the great night arrived. It was 2 A.M. when the first puppy was born. The tiny creature emerged headfirst, covered in its birth sac. Mistel licked it to help break the sac and then bit through the *umbilical cord*. She seemed to know exactly what she was doing.

Puppy after puppy arrived, 30 minutes apart. Alex could hardly believe his eyes. Eight puppies was an average litter, and Mistel had given birth to a lucky 13! Using the kitchen scale, Alex weighed one of the pups. Because the litter was large, the pup was small for a Doberman. It weighed 14 ounces. All the puppies' eyes were closed, and he knew they'd be deaf for nearly ten days.

Mrs. Ford came in to sit with him. "Mistel only has ten *teats*," she said. "The smallest pups will go hungry if we don't do some hand feeding. Is there anything else to do?"

"I'll ask Dr. Vincent to come in to dock their tails on the fourth day," Alex said. "He can look them over, and he'll check Mistel, too. Look at how she's licking each one to clean and warm it. Isn't she a great mother!"

Watching Dr. Vincent docking the puppies' tails was upsetting to Alex. He felt better when he saw the pups didn't seem to suffer very much. After that experience, Alex decided not to have their ears cropped. Two weeks later, the puppies were rambling around on wobbly legs, squealing and yapping. At

A Schutzhund must show excellent obedience, tracking, and protection skills.

four weeks, Mistel began *weaning* them. Alex knew it was time to start looking for buyers.

The last puppy was sold three months later. The house seemed lifeless with all 13 puppies gone. Alex sighed and took Mistel for a long run. His bankbook showed a profit of only $250 for six months' work, but he felt wonderful.

"Raising puppies was great," he said. "Do you want to try again next year?" Mistel barked once and licked his face.

TRAINING TO BE A SCHUTZHUND

Most dog shows are beauty contests. The judging is based on how well the dog meets the highest standards of its breed. Obedience is expected, but dogs win Best of Breed for their looks.

Owners who aren't interested in beauty contests enter their Dobermans in obedience trials. Obedience competition rates dogs on what they can do, not on how they look. Because Dobermans were bred to be working dogs, they do well in these contests. In a typical trial, the dogs must obey all commands instantly, on and off the leash. The most talented Dobermans compete in the *Schutzhund* competitions. (*Schutzhund* is German for guard dog.) A dog must show superior ability in obedience, tracking, and protection to win this ranking. Any dog taller than 18 inches at the withers can be entered.

In order to earn the Schutzhund I degree (SchH I), a Doberman must pass three trials. Each trial is worth 100 points, and a dog needs 220 points to qualify. In tracking, the dog must follow an unmarked trail laid down by its handler. The handler drops two objects along the way, which the dog must find. In the obedience section, the dog must work on and off the leash. At one point, while the dog is off the leash, a gun is fired. If the dog shies away from the noise, it fails the entire trial. Retrieving objects, making a 39-inch high jump, and staying in place are also part of the obedience trials.

Finally, in protection work, the dog must locate a decoy hiding in a field. The person playing the role of the decoy wears padded clothing. When the dog finds the decoy, it must bark but not bite. In a second exercise, the dog must attack when the decoy attacks its handler. The dog should be fearless, but it must control its aggression on command.

The best dogs can go on to qualify as Schutzhunds II and III. Each level puts the dogs through more difficult tests. Top dogs can go on to take an endurance exam. In this test, the dogs must cover 12 miles at an average speed of 6 miles per hour. Only three rest stops are allowed. The handlers don't have to be marathon runners—they're allowed to cover the course on bicycles.

During an obedience trial, Dobermans must retrieve an object and make a 39-inch high jump.

A CRIME FIGHTER

Everyone knows Doberman pinschers make excellent watchdogs, right? Any dog that can earn a Schutzhund degree must be good. What many people don't know is that some of the nation's largest department stores are guarded by Dobermans.

The stores turned to Dobermans to solve a long series of thefts. Thieves were entering the stores and mixing with the customers. Just before closing time, they disappeared. That was easy, because department stores have thousands of good hiding places. After all the clerks left, the thieves waited until the guards went to another floor. When the way was clear, they picked up jewelry and other small items. Then they went back into hiding. When the store opened for business the next morning, the thieves strolled out with their loot.

Macy's department store in New York City hit on a way to solve the problem. Instead of hiring more security guards, the store "hired" four Doberman guard dogs. Each dog was trained to patrol the store at night with a security guard. If the dog found hidden thieves, it flushed the intruders and held them. No hiding place was safe from these canine patrols, and the number of thefts fell at once. The Doberman patrol also paid off in other ways. The dogs spotted overheated machines, leaking pipes, and smoldering fires.

The Doberman's keen nose has paid off in other ways, too. The U.S. Customs Service uses dogs to sniff out drugs and other illegal materials. A Doberman can find cocaine that's been wrapped with heavy plastic and embedded in plaster. The Department of Agriculture

The Doberman's watchdog qualities have been useful in catching drug smugglers and department store thieves.

uses its dogs to keep illegal plants from entering the United States. The fruit carried by a tourist may look harmless, but it can carry pests such as the Oriental fruit fly. The Doberman's successful police work puts the breed on the front line in the war against disease and crime.

WHY DOES A DOBERMAN BARK?

You're walking down the street, minding your own business. Suddenly, a Doberman pinscher rushes at you. Only the fence stands between you and the angry dog. You back away, alarmed by the barking and the sight of those sharp teeth. You like dogs, but this one is scary.

Dog trainers tell us that a barking dog is sounding a warning. In dog language, the Doberman is calling, "Hey, Boss, listen to me! A stranger is invading our territory!" If you think like a dog for a moment, it makes sense. In the Doberman's mind, its owners are its pack and its yard is the pack's territory. Both must be protected. But unless you threaten the dog or invade its yard, it probably won't do more than bark at you.

The Doberman pinscher that barked at you was doing what comes naturally. It's the dog that charges *without barking* that you should fear. Let's say you're selling raffle tickets, and you start toward someone's front door. You don't know a Doberman lives there. The dog comes toward you, mouth open and snarling. It's walking stifflegged and the hair on its neck is raised. The message is clear: "You're on my turf, and it's my job to drive you away."

How do you keep from being bitten? Don't run! Stand your ground and talk soothingly to the Doberman. Don't move suddenly and try not to show any fear. Hold your bike, your books, or your coat between you and the dog. If you're successful, the dog will realize you're not a threat. The snarling will give way to growling and barking. The new sounds mean, "I'd like to attack, but I'm not sure I should. I'll sound the alarm instead." Back away slowly. Don't turn your back on the dog until you're sure it won't follow you.

Dobermans share a "language" common to all dogs. If you listen carefully, you can understand what a barking or growling dog is telling you.

THE DOBERMAN GOES TO WAR

In November 1943, American forces in World War II landed on the Japanese-held island of Bougainville. The marines set up a beachhead, but the jungle fighting was fierce. One platoon pushed ahead, only to be pinned down by Japanese machine-gun fire. No one could tell where the enemy was located. Bullets seemed to be whizzing by from all directions.

Luckily, the Marine Corps had adopted the Doberman as its official dog. These marines had a Doberman with them named Andy. Guided by hand signals from his handler, Andy quickly helped the marines spot the machine-gun nests. Knowing the enemy's position turned the tide of battle. The marines cleaned out the machine guns and moved on to their next objective.

Andy almost didn't get to be a hero. When the war started in 1941, many Americans thought dogs would eat food needed for the war effort. "Let's get rid of the lot of them,"

During World War II, Dobermans were trained to assist soldiers by tracking escaped prisoners and searching for booby traps.

the antidog people said. Dog lovers quickly pointed out that dogs had been used in war since ancient times. Dogs could free men to fight by guarding factories and military camps. After air raids, they could search out people who were trapped in bombed buildings. Most of all, they could fight alongside the soldiers.

An organization called Dogs for Defense was formed to collect and train "war dogs." Dog owners rushed to volunteer their pets. The War Department saw the value of using dogs and set up training camps across the United States. At first, over 30 breeds were accepted for war duty. Later, the military favored Dobermans and German shepherds over the other breeds. War dogs had to be between one and five years old. They had to weigh over 50 pounds and measure at least 20 inches at the withers. In a play on words, the dogs were called the K-9 Corps (instead of the Canine Corps).

By the end of the war, over 250,000 dogs had served in the armed forces. Dobermans and other dogs were trained to several types of duty. Commando dogs were the all-around K-9 stars. A commando dog obeyed commands given by voice, by touch, or by silent whistle.

These dogs could do sentry duty, track escaping prisoners, scout hostile positions, and attack enemy soldiers. Assault dogs were used to flush out enemy troops from foxholes, caves, and jungle hideouts. Patrol dogs went out with their handlers to scout enemy positions. Their sharp noses and ears often detected dangers that the soldiers hadn't seen. Sentry dogs joined soldiers in guarding camps or outposts. Sentry dogs never barked. They tugged on their handler's sleeves to warn of danger. Perhaps the riskiest job of all was given to mine-detector dogs. These dogs sniffed out mines and booby traps that were set to kill advancing soldiers.

The dogs did their work well, but the price was high. Of the first eight dogs shipped to the South Pacific, for example, none returned. Five were killed while on duty, and the others died of disease. After the war, many dogs were retrained and sent back to their old homes. There was still work for dogs to do, however. Dogs for Defense took on the job of furnishing puppies to military hospitals. The lively young dogs helped cheer lonely veterans who had been wounded during the war. People had finally realized the importance—and friendliness—of Doberman pinschers.

▌GLOSSARY/INDEX

Bitch 24—An adult female dog.

Breeding 8, 13, 20, 23, 31, 35—To mate a quality bitch with a quality male.

Canines 14—The four long, sharp holding teeth in the front of a dog's mouth.

Carnivore 11—A meat-eating animal.

Choke Chain 27—A leash made from heavy metal links that is used in training a dog.

Crop 14, 15, 25, 33—To cut away part of the earflap so that the remaining ear will stand erect.

Crossbred 9 — Two different breeds of dog mated in hopes that the puppies will combine the best qualities of each.

Distemper 29—A serious disease that affects puppies.

Dock 14, 33—To shorten a dog's tail by cutting it off at the first or second joint.

Forelegs 15—The front legs of an animal.

Grooming 28, 29—Brushing a dog to keep its coat clean and smooth.

Guard Dog 9, 14, 19, 21, 23, 38—A dog that's been trained to protect people and property.

Haw 17—The dog's third eyelid.

Heat 18, 24, 32—The time when a bitch is ready to mate.

Housebreaking 27—Training a puppy so it doesn't relieve itself inside the house.

46

GLOSSARY/INDEX

Incisors 14—The nipping and cutting teeth that grow between the canines.

Instincts 9, 27—Natural behavior that is inborn in a dog.

Litter 22, 25, 32, 33—A family of puppies born at a single whelping.

Molars 14—The dog's back teeth, used for slicing and crushing.

Muzzle 13—The part of the head that includes the mouth, jaws, and nose of an animal.

Obedience Trial 6, 35, 36—A competition in which dogs are judged on how well they obey a series of commands.

Olfactory Patches 17—The nerve endings in the nose that provide a dog's keen sense of smell.

Pedigree 23, 31—A chart that lists a dog's ancestors.

Premolars 14—A dog's back teeth, used for slicing and chewing.

Puppy 9, 14, 15, 17, 22, 23, 24, 25, 26, 28, 31, 32, 33, 34, 45—A dog under one year of age.

Reinforce 26—To encourage and reward a dog when it obeys a command.

Schutzhund 35, 36, 38—A first-class guard dog. A Doberman earns this ranking by passing a series of difficult obedience, tracking, and protection trials.

GLOSSARY/INDEX

Show Dog 23—A dog that meets the highest standards of its breed.

Stud Male 31—A purebred male used for breeding.

Teats 33—The female dog's nipples. Puppies suck on the teats to get milk.

Umbilical Cord 33—The hollow tube that carries nutrients to the puppy while it's inside the mother's body.

Veterinarian 15, 25, 28, 29, 30—A doctor who is trained to take care of animals.

Weaning 34—The time when a puppy stops nursing from its mother.

Whelping 32—The birth of a litter of puppies.

Withers 13, 15, 35, 44—The dog's shoulder, the point where its neck joins the body. A dog's height is measured at the withers.

Worms 29—Dangerous parasites that live in a dog's intestines.